A DK PUBLISHING BOOK

Written by Mary Atkinson
Art Editor Mandy Earey
Deputy Managing Editor Dawn Sirett
Deputy Managing Art Editor
C. David Gillingwater
US Editor Camela Decaire
Production Josie Alabaster
Picture Research Jennifer Silkstone
and Angela Anderson

First American Edition, 1997
2 4 6 8 10 9 7 5 3 1
Published in the United States by
DK Publishing, Inc., 95 Madison Avenue, New York, New York 10016
Visit us on the World Wide Web at http://www.dk.com

Copyright © 1997 Dorling Kindersley Limited, London

A CIP catalog record for this book is
available from the Library of Congress.

ISBN 0-7894-2055-4

Color reproduction by Chromagraphics, Singapore
Printed and bound in Italy by L.E.G.O.

The publisher would like to thank the following for their kind
permission to reproduce their photographs:

t=top, b=bottom, l=left, r=right, c=center, BC=back cover, FC=front cover

Ace Photo Agency: Jigsaw (Why did Grandpa die?)c; **Format Photographers**: Jenny
Matthews (Why do I have to go ...?)c; **Robert Harding Picture Library**: FC ctr,
endpapers, (Why do grown-ups get ....?)br, (Why do I have a new stepbrother?)c,
The Image Bank: Elyse Lewin (Why do we have so many ...?)tr, (Why do some
parents ..?)br, Marc Romanelli (Why doesn't Grandma ...?)bl; **Images Colour Library**
(Why doesn't Grandma ...?)c; **Tony Stone Images**: Ken Fisher BC c, Walter Hodges
(Why do we live ...?)c, Bruce Ayres (Why do grown-ups get ...?)c, Graeme Harris
(Why did Grandpa die?)tr, Howard Grey (Why do some parents ..?)c; **Zefa**: FC cbr,
FC ctl, (Why do we live ...?)tl, (Why do we live ...?)br, (Why do we have so
many ...?)bl, (Why do some parents ..?)tl, FC cbl, (Why do I have a new stepbrother?)tr.

Additional photography by Paul Bricknell, Jo Foord, Steve Gorton,
Dave King, Ray Moller, Susannah Price, and Steve Shott.

Questions

Why do we live in families?

Why do we have so many relatives?

Why do grown-ups get angry sometimes?

Why do I have to go to bed early?

Why doesn't Grandma go to work anymore?

Why did Grandpa die?

Why do some parents split up?

Why do I have a new stepbrother?

3

WHY

are all families different?

Questions children ask
about families

Consultant: Diane Melvin, Clinical Child Psychologist

DK

DK PUBLISHING, INC.

Why do we live

It's usually the people in our family who take care of us and teach us about the world as we grow up. Our parents,

Why are all families different?

All families are different because all people are different. Some people want lots of children, others want just one child. The members of a family are usually related by birth and can include half brothers and sisters. Many families have only one parent, and some members of a family may be adopted.

in families?

brothers, sisters, and other
relatives love us and watch
over us. They do their best to
help us grow up happy.

**Why are people who live
far away part of my family?**
When we talk about our
family we often mean the
people who live with us.
Yet our relatives such as
our cousins, aunts, uncles,
and grandparents are all
part of our bigger family,
even if they live abroad.

Why do we have so many

Most people are connected to lots of other people by birth – aunts, uncles, cousins, and grandparents. We can draw a diagram joining up our relatives. It's called a family tree, and it shows how everyone is related to everyone else.

Why do I have aunts and uncles?
Your aunts and uncles are usually your parents' sisters and brothers and their partners. Sometimes we also call a close family friend our uncle or aunt.

Emma's Family Tree

Lorna and H
Emma's grandpa

Linda
Emma's mother

Michael
Emma's father

Matthew
Emma's brother

Emma

relatives?

Eddy and Edith
Emma's grandparents

Joanna
Emma's aunt

Suzy
Emma's aunt

Stephen
Emma's uncle

...tie
...sister

Jack
Emma's cousin

Why does my mom call my grandma Mom?
Your grandparents are your mom and dad's parents. One set of your grandparents is your mom's mom and dad, and the other set is your dad's mom and dad. Not everyone knows all their grandparents. Some grandparents are no longer alive when their grandchildren are growing up.

Grown-ups can get angry when we're bad, and they may also get upset at other times. Just like you, they have different moods. They may be irritable because they're feeling tired or because they've had a hard day.

Why do my mom and dad tell me to go away and play?

When grown-ups tell you to go and play, they still love you,

get angry sometimes?

Why do I want my mom and dad when I'm upset?
The people who love us and take care of us also help us get through bad times. When things go wrong, a hug or a talk with someone in our family or with a trusted friend can often help us feel better again.

they just need some quiet time to themselves. They may want to rest or to concentrate on their work for a little while.

Why do I have to go to

Young children need more
sleep than adults. While
you're asleep, your body
does much of its growing,

**Why should I share my toys
with my brother and sister?**
Think how you feel when
someone won't share with you.
Letting others play with your
toys makes them happy. It also
means you have friends to
play with and, afterward, the
toys are still yours to keep.

bed early?

and stores up energy for the next day. As you get older, you will be able to stay up later.

Why do I have to clean up when I'm done playing?
In a family, everyone helps with the work. When you were a baby you were too young to do much. But now that you're bigger, you can help keep your home neat by putting away your toys. After all, no one enjoys cleaning up someone else's mess.

Why doesn't Grandma

Why did Mom want to have another baby?

Many parents want another baby because they want a bigger family. In just a few years, the baby will grow to be a friend and playmate for the children they already have, and everyone can enjoy caring for it and getting to know it.

As our bodies grow older, we find it harder to work all day, which is why most older people stop going to work.

go to work anymore?

This is called retiring. Some retired people enjoy spending their free time with their children and grandchildren.

Why has Dad stopped going to work?
Few people stay in the same job all their lives. Some people decide to try a different job. Others lose their job when a workplace needs less people. Finding a new job can take time. The right job is not always readily available.

As people grow older, their bodies start to wear out, and eventually they die. Often, we miss them very much and feel sad inside. But we never forget them, and, in time, we come to enjoy thinking about the good times we had with them.

Why did my best friend move away?
Families move for all sorts of reasons. They may need a bigger home, or want to be near a new workplace. Although we miss our friends when they move away, we can keep in touch with letters, phone calls, or even visits.

die?

Why won't my big sister play with me anymore?

Just like you don't want to play with babies' toys anymore, bigger children grow out of many of the games that you still enjoy. They have fun doing more grown-up activities, and they also have a lot more homework to do!

Why do some

Even parents are still learning. Sometimes two people find that they want to live their lives in different ways. This

Why do I see Daddy only on weekends?
Parents who no longer live together both still want to be with their children. One way to do this is for the children to see one parent on weekends and the other one during the week.

parents split up?

may mean that they live
apart. However, they both
still love their children just
as much as they ever did.

**Why doesn't Daddy
come back if I
promise to be good?**
When parents split up
it is not because of
anything their children
have done. Whether
your parents are pleased
with you or angry with you,
they will always love you.

When two people who already have children get married, their children become stepbrothers and -sisters. Sometimes all the children share a home, and, in time, they often become good friends.

Why do I have a new parent?
Sometimes after children's parents split up, one of them meets someone else they love and want to be with. That person may become the children's stepfather or -mother. It takes time to get used to a new parent and to enjoy being with them.

new stepbrother?

Why was I adopted?
When the birth parents of a child are unable to take care of it themselves, the child may be cared for by another family. The child might live with a couple that wants children very much, but can't have any naturally. The child's new parents take care of it and love it for the rest of their lives.